www.mascotbooks.com

Glory Days Press™ Sports Biographies: Tom Brady

For more information, please contact:
Mascot Books
560 Herndon Parkway #120
Herndon, VA 20170
info@mascotbooks.com

CPSIA Code: PRT0217A
Library of Congress Control Number: 2016920339
ISBN-13: 978-1-68401-013-4

Printed in the United States

GLORY DAYS
PRESS

SPORTS BIOGRAPHIES
TOM BRADY

ANDREA ALEXANDER

illustrated by
JASON BUHAGIAR

NOTE TO PARENTS

Kids hear about professional athletes all the time, and they get excited about the player or sport. *Glory Days Press™* wants to couple that enthusiasm with reading and provide books on players that capture their interest.

Kids who love sports know their athletes and want to learn everything about them. By providing a selection of books on topics that appeal to kids, our hope is they realize the benefits of reading, reinforce their vocabulary, and look forward to the next book.

-Andrea

Thomas Edward Patrick Brady, Jr. was born
August 3, 1977, in San Mateo, California.

Tom attended St. Gregory's Elementary School and
played many different sports, including soccer,
basketball, and baseball. He also enjoyed golfing
on Sundays with his dad.

Like most kids, Tom had a huge collection
of baseball cards!

Growing up, Tom and his sisters constantly competed against each other, and they'd often have water gun fights in the backyard!

Tom has three older sisters, Maureen, Nancy, and Julie, who also excelled in sports. As the youngest sibling, he was known to most people as "The Little Brady."

The Brady family attended nearly every home game of the San Francisco 49ers, and that's where Tom found his love for football. He grew up a 49ers fan and always looked forward to watching Joe Montana.

Tom went to San Mateo's Junipero Serra High School, an all-boys Catholic school, where he played tackle football for the first time. By his junior year, he earned the starting quarterback position for the Padres!

Tom played varsity football, basketball, and baseball in high school.

Tom's high school football coach introduced the five-dot drill to increase foot speed and agility. While many players dreaded it, Tom worked on it constantly. He even spray-painted five dots on his parents' patio so he could perform the drill every day!

During his high school career, Tom completed 236 of 447 passes for 3,702 yards and 31 touchdowns. He also won All-State and All-Far West honors, as well as the team's MVP!

After high school, Tom took off to Ann Arbor, Michigan, to play for the Wolverines.

But Tom wasn't just good at football. He was an excellent catcher for his high school baseball team, too. He was so good at baseball that the Montreal Expos selected him in the eighteenth round of the 1995 MLB draft! Even though he knew it was a great opportunity, he chose to head to the University of Michigan to continue playing the game he loved most—football!

By his junior year, Tom became the starting quarterback, throwing 350 passes for 2,636 yards. He earned an All-Big Ten Conference honorable mention and was selected for the Academic All-Big Ten team. He also set several University of Michigan records, including the record for most attempts and completions in one season with 350 and 214!

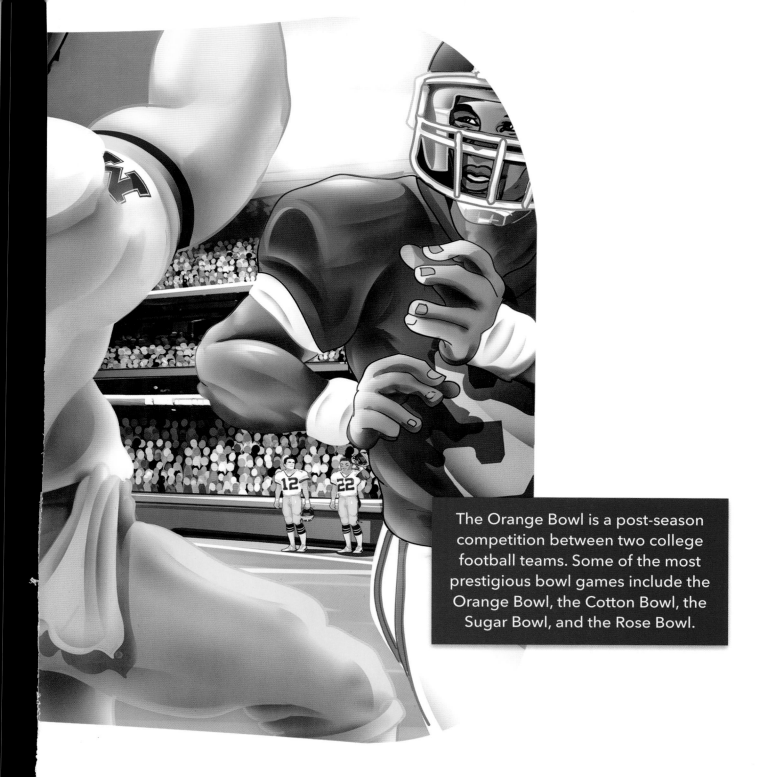

The Orange Bowl is a post-season competition between two college football teams. Some of the most prestigious bowl games include the Orange Bowl, the Cotton Bowl, the Sugar Bowl, and the Rose Bowl.

In his last season at Michigan, Tom was team captain and led the Wolverines to an Orange Bowl victory over the University of Alabama. He threw for 369 yards and had 4 touchdowns, defeating Alabama 35-34 in overtime!

Tom Brady
University of Michigan

443 completions

62.3 completion percentage

5,351 passing yards

35 passing touchdowns

Tom set several school records at the University of Michigan.

While at college, Tom won 20 of the 25 games he started!

During the 2000 NFL draft, the New England Patriots
selected Tom in the sixth round.

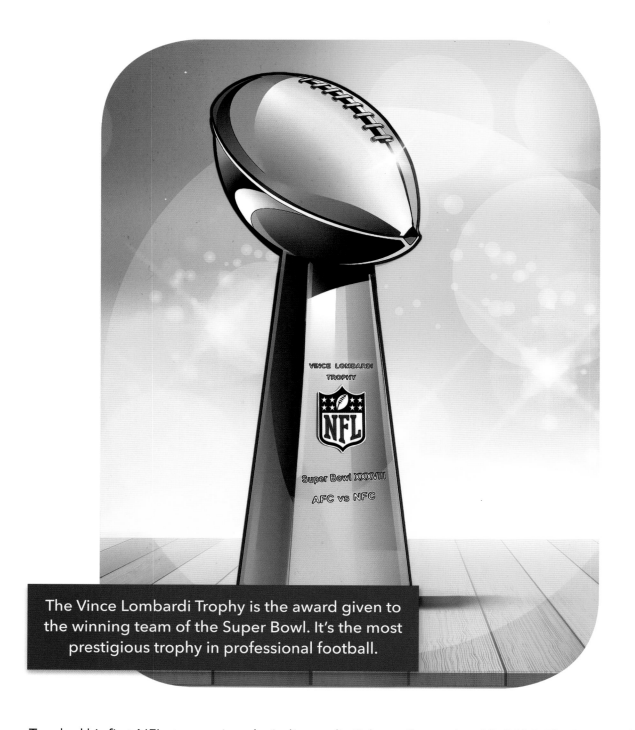

The Vince Lombardi Trophy is the award given to the winning team of the Super Bowl. It's the most prestigious trophy in professional football.

Tom had his first NFL start against the Indianapolis Colts on September 30, 2001. The Patriots defeated the Colts in a 44-13 victory, and Tom threw for 168 yards with 13 completions and 23 attempts.

By 2002, Tom became the then-youngest quarterback in NFL history to lead his team to a Super Bowl victory! The Patriots defeated the St. Louis Rams 20-17, and Tom earned his first Super Bowl MVP award!

Each player of the winning team receives a Super Bowl ring to keep as a memento of their victory. The team name, team logo, and Super Bowl number are typically included.

Just two years later, Tom brought the Patriots back to the Super Bowl for a victory over the Carolina Panthers 32-29! For a second time, Tom received the Super Bowl MVP award.

In 2005, the Patriots followed up as AFC East champions and back-to-back Super Bowl champions!

DATE	OPPONENT	FINAL SCORE	PATRIOTS RECORD
Sep 9, 2007	NEW YORK JETS	38-14	1-0
Sep 16, 2007	SAN DIEGO CHARGERS	38-14	2-0
Sep 23, 2007	BUFFALO BILLS	38-7	3-0
Oct 1, 2007	CINCINNATI BENGALS	34-13	4-0
Oct 7, 2007	CLEVELAND BROWNS	34-17	5-0
Oct 4, 2007	DALLAS COWBOYS	48-27	6-0
Oct 21, 2007	MIAMI DOLPHINS	49-28	7-0
Oct 8, 2007	WASHINGTON REDSKINS	52-7	8-0
Nov 4, 2007	INDIANAPOLIS COLTS	24-20	9-0
Nov 18, 2007	BUFFALO BILLS	56-10	10-0
Nov 25, 2007	PHILADELPHIA EAGLES	31-28	11-0
Dec 3, 2007	BALTIMORE RAVENS	27-24	12-0
Dec 9, 2007	PITTSBURGH STEELERS	34-13	13-0
Dec 16, 2007	NEW YORK JETS	20-10	14-0
Dec 23, 2007	MIAMI DOLPHINS	28-7	15-0
Dec 29, 2007	NEW YORK GIANTS	38-35	16-0

Tom went on to lead the team in several winning seasons, and the Patriots even went undefeated in the 2007 regular season to become the AFC champions!

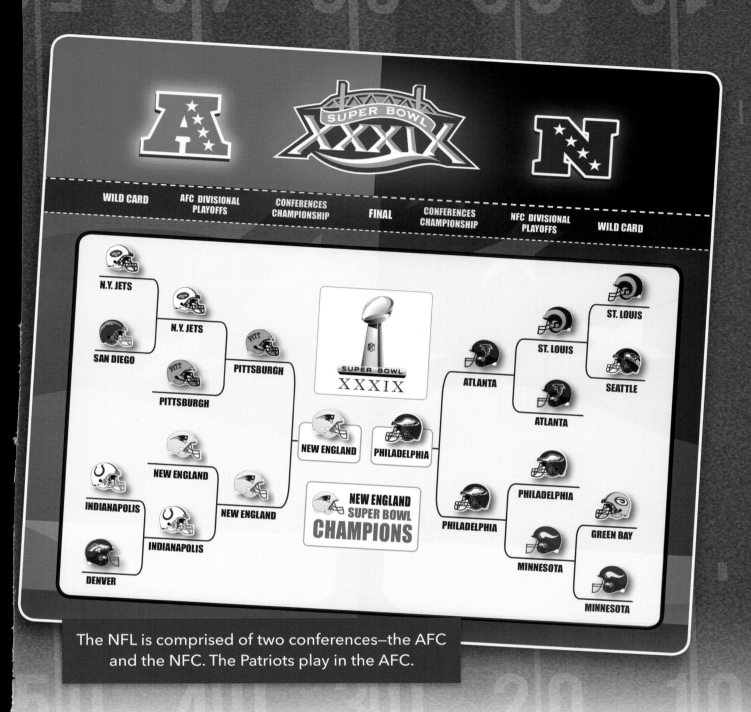

WILD CARD · AFC DIVISIONAL PLAYOFFS · CONFERENCES CHAMPIONSHIP · FINAL · CONFERENCES CHAMPIONSHIP · NFC DIVISIONAL PLAYOFFS · WILD CARD

N.Y. JETS
N.Y. JETS
SAN DIEGO
PITTSBURGH
PITTSBURGH
PITTSBURGH

NEW ENGLAND
NEW ENGLAND
INDIANAPOLIS
INDIANAPOLIS
NEW ENGLAND
DENVER

NEW ENGLAND   PHILADELPHIA

SUPER BOWL XXXIX

NEW ENGLAND SUPER BOWL CHAMPIONS

ATLANTA
ST. LOUIS
ST. LOUIS
SEATTLE
ATLANTA
ATLANTA

PHILADELPHIA
PHILADELPHIA
MINNESOTA
GREEN BAY
MINNESOTA

The NFL is comprised of two conferences—the AFC and the NFC. The Patriots play in the AFC.

Due to injuries, Tom wasn't able to play during the 2008 season but came back strong the next year! The Patriots went 10-6 during the 2009 season and had an even better record of 14-2 the next year!

16

In 2011, Tom led the team to a 13-3 regular season record and made his fourth Super Bowl appearance against the New York Giants. With another close game, the Giants beat the Patriots 21-17.

In 2014, the Patriots finished 12-4 for the third year in a row and won the sixth consecutive AFC East title! They went on to defeat the Indianapolis Colts 45-7 for the AFC championship and appeared, once again, in the Super Bowl!

On February 1, 2015, the Patriots played the Seattle Seahawks in Super Bowl XLIX. After being down 10 points in the second half, they rallied in the final quarter to win 28-24!

On February 5, 2017, Tom steered his team to defeat the Atlanta Falcons in Super Bowl LI. Down 21-3 at the half, the New England Patriots rallied to win 34-28 in the first overtime in Super Bowl history. Tom threw for 466 yards and was once again named the MVP!

The Pro Football Hall of Fame is located in Canton, Ohio. Players must be retired five years before they are eligible to be voted in.

Tom Brady has led the New England Patriots to numerous Super Bowl victories and is considered one of the greatest quarterbacks to ever play the game. Through his hard work, determination, and fierce competitive spirit, there's no doubt he will one day end up in the Pro Football Hall of Fame!

FUN FACTS ON TOM BRADY!

When Tom was in college, he told his roommate that his dream was to make enough money one day so he could put on a new pair of socks every morning and be able to throw them out at the end of the day.

Avocado ice cream is one of Tom's favorite desserts!

Tom keeps coconut water in his locker for when he's thirsty!

Tom was outside playing baseball with his dad when he got the call that he had been drafted by the Patriots!

Tom once lived in a house that had a moat!

Tom played catcher in high school.

FOOTBALL LINGO

AFC – The American Football Conference is one of the two conferences of the National Football League (NFL).

Down – A single play. Teams are given four downs to advance the ball ten yards, resulting in another first down.

End Zone – The end of the field where the team with the ball can score a touchdown.

Extra Point – The kick that takes place after a team scores a touchdown. If successful, the team gets another point.

False Start – When an offensive player moves before the ball is snapped.

Flag – What referees throw to signal a penalty has taken place during the play.

Flea Flicker – When the quarterback hands the ball off to a player to then have it tossed back to him.

Fumble – When a player loses control of the football and it is recovered by another player.

Hail Mary – An effort at the very end of a game to score. The quarterback throws a long pass into the end zone hoping for the touchdown.

Holding – When a player's progress is stopped or impeded by being held illegally by an opposing player.

Icing – When the opposing coach calls a late timeout as the kicker is attempting a field goal.

Line of Scrimmage – The yard line where the play or down begins.

NFC – The National Football Conference is one of the two conferences of the National Football League (NFL).

NFL – The professional American football league consisting of thirty-two teams, divided equally between the NFC and the AFC. The NFL is the highest professional level of American football.

Offside – When the defense crosses the line of scrimmage before the ball is snapped.

Pickoff – An intercepted pass.

Pig Skin – The football. The first footballs were made of inflated pig bladders (yuck!).

Quarterback Sneak – When the quarterback unexpectedly runs the ball.

Scramble – When a quarterback moves around a lot to avoid the pass rush.

Straight/Stiff Arm – When a ball carrier uses the arm he's not using to carry the ball to fend off defenders.

Two-Point Conversion – After a touchdown is scored, the team can kick a field goal for an extra point or they can attempt a two-point conversion. To get a two-point conversion, they must get the ball into the end zone from the two-yard line.

COLLECT THEM ALL!

✂ cut here

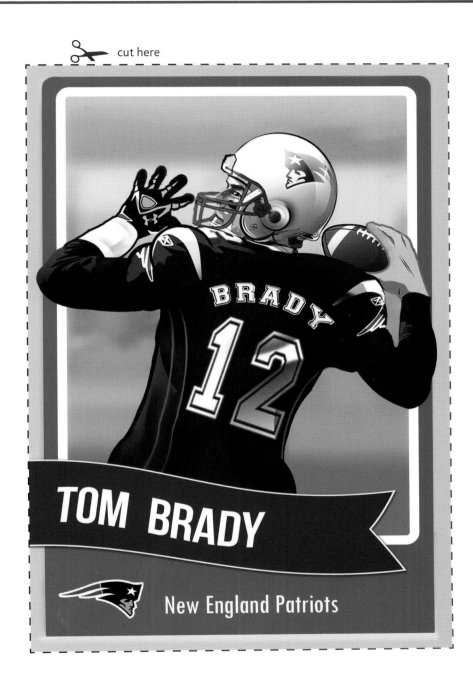

4 TOM BRADY

HEIGHT: 6'4"   BORN: 8/3/77
WEIGHT: 225 lbs.   FROM: San Mateo, CA
POSITION: Quarterback DRAFTED: 2000

2016 SEASON STATS

Games Played:	12
Completions:	291
Pass Attempts:	432
Completion %:	67.4
Yards:	3,554
Yards Per Pass Attempt:	8.2
Touchdowns:	28

OTHER BOOKS BY *GLORY DAYS PRESS*™

COMING SOON FROM *GLORY DAYS PRESS*™

SUBMIT YOUR
FAVORITE ATHLETE

andrea@glorydayspress.com | www.glorydayspress.com